Learn to Read wit Week Orton Gillingham Decodable Readers Plan

A Workbook for Overcoming Dyslexia in Struggling Readers

Orton Gillingham Materials

Week 4

BrainChild

WHAT IS THE APPROACH

The Orton-Gillingham Approach is a highly effective, research-based method for teaching reading that has transformed the educational experiences of countless individuals, especially those with dyslexia and other reading difficulties. This approach is distinguished by its multisensory, structured, sequential, and phonics-based methodology, designed to adapt to the unique needs of each learner.

At its core, the Orton-Gillingham Approach integrates visual, auditory, and kinesthetic-tactile cues to help students understand the alphabetic code and master the intricacies of the English language. This multisensory aspect ensures that learning is more engaging and accessible, catering to various learning styles and making the reading process more concrete for those who struggle with traditional methods.

The structure of the Orton-Gillingham Approach is meticulous and deliberate, following a precise and systematic progression. Lessons begin with the simplest concepts and gradually move towards more complex aspects of language, ensuring that each step is firmly understood before advancing. This careful sequencing helps build a solid foundation, enabling learners to accumulate skills in a logical order which enhances their reading capabilities and confidence.

Phonics is another cornerstone of this approach, emphasizing the relationship between sounds and their corresponding letters or letter groups. By focusing on phonemic awareness, students are equipped to decode words independently, an essential skill for fluent reading and spelling.

The Orton-Gillingham Approach is also characterized by its flexibility and individualized instruction. Recognizing that every learner's journey is unique, it advocates for personalized lesson plans that are tailored to the student's specific challenges, strengths, pace, and interests. This personalized attention not only improves reading skills but also nurtures a positive attitude towards learning.

By addressing the root causes of reading difficulties with an empathetic, evidence-based strategy, the Orton-Gillingham Approach offers a powerful solution for those who have found traditional reading instruction challenging. Its effectiveness lies in its ability to demystify the reading process, providing learners with the tools they need to achieve success and fostering a lifelong love for reading.

GOALS

Welcome to "The 8-Week Orton-Gillingham Decodable Readers Plan," a transformative guide designed to revolutionize the reading journey for individuals facing challenges with dyslexia and other reading difficulties. Rooted in the proven principles of the Orton-Gillingham approach, this book is crafted with the singular goal of making reading accessible, enjoyable, and rewarding for everyone.

Purpose of the Book:

The primary purpose of this book is to provide a structured, step-by-step plan that harnesses the power of decodable readers in conjunction with the multisensory, structured, sequential, and phonics-based methodologies of the Orton-Gillingham approach. By focusing on these elements, we aim to tackle the complexities of reading head-on, transforming what often feels like an insurmountable challenge into an achievable goal.

Goals of the 8-Week Plan:

- **To Improve Reading Skills:** Through a carefully curated selection of decodable readers, this plan offers a progressive series of texts that align with the learner's developing skills. By gradually increasing complexity, we ensure a smooth escalation of reading proficiency, catering to the learner's pace and ensuring solid grounding before moving forward.

- **To Enhance Understanding of Phonics:** Phonemic awareness is crucial for decoding and fluency. This book emphasizes phonics instruction through engaging activities and targeted exercises, reinforcing the connection between sounds and symbols, which is essential for readers with dyslexia.

- **To Build Confidence in Struggling Readers:** Confidence plays a significant role in overcoming reading difficulties. By providing achievable milestones and celebrating progress, this plan aims to bolster self-esteem and foster a positive attitude towards reading. The inclusivity and adaptability of the Orton-Gillingham approach ensure that each learner feels supported and understood.

Expected Outcomes:

Upon completing the 8-week plan, readers can expect to see significant improvements in their reading abilities. Specific outcomes include:

- Enhanced ability to decode words independently and accurately.
- Improved reading fluency and comprehension.
- A stronger foundation in phonics and word recognition.
- Increased confidence and motivation to read.
- A deeper appreciation for the joy of reading.

"The 8-Week Orton-Gillingham Decodable Readers Plan" is more than just a book; it's a journey towards reading success. Whether you're an educator seeking effective strategies, a parent supporting your child at home, or an adult learner embarking on your own reading journey, this book offers the tools, guidance, and encouragement needed to unlock the full potential of every reader.

FOR WHOM IS THIS BOOK

"The 8-Week Orton-Gillingham Decodable Readers Plan" is designed to cater to a diverse audience, each with a vested interest in overcoming reading difficulties through an effective, structured approach. This book is particularly beneficial for:

Educators:

Teachers and special education professionals will find this book an invaluable resource for structured literacy instruction. It serves as a comprehensive guide to implementing the Orton-Gillingham approach in the classroom, offering a clear, week-by-week plan that can be adapted to the needs of individual students or small groups. Educators seeking evidence-based strategies to support students with dyslexia or other reading challenges will discover a wealth of activities, exercises, and decodable texts to enhance their teaching repertoire.

Parents and Guardians:

For parents and guardians looking to support their children's reading journey at home, this book provides a straightforward, manageable approach. Whether supplementing school-based learning or homeschooling, the plan offers a structured path to improving reading skills, with activities designed to engage children in a supportive, nurturing environment. It empowers parents with the tools and knowledge to effectively assist their children, making it an ideal resource for families committed to overcoming reading difficulties together.

Adult Learners:

Adults facing reading challenges, including those with dyslexia, will find this book a practical and encouraging guide to improving their reading skills. The 8-week plan offers a structured yet flexible approach, allowing adult learners to progress at their own pace. With clear instructions, engaging materials, and activities tailored to adult readers, this book helps demystify reading, providing a pathway to greater confidence and proficiency.

Tutors and Therapists:

Reading tutors and speech-language therapists will appreciate the book's systematic, evidence-based approach to reading intervention. Its detailed plan supports one-on-one tutoring sessions and therapy, offering a rich source of activities and strategies tailored to the needs of individual learners. The book's focus on the Orton-Gillingham approach ensures that professionals are equipped with effective tools to help learners overcome reading barriers.

In essence, "The 8-Week Orton-Gillingham Decodable Readers Plan" is suited to anyone committed to improving reading skills through a structured, multisensory approach. By clearly defining its target audience, the book ensures that readers can quickly assess its relevance to their personal, educational, or professional needs, promising a pathway to reading success for a wide range of individuals.

"The 8-Week Orton-Gillingham Decodable Readers Plan" is a meticulously structured program designed to systematically enhance reading skills through a series of targeted activities, exercises, and reading materials. Each week focuses on specific phonetic concepts, building upon the previous lessons to solidify reading foundations and advance learners' abilities. Here's an overview of the structure and progression throughout the eight weeks:

Week 1: Mastering CVC Words (Volume 1)

- **Focus:** Introduction to consonant-vowel-consonant (CVC) words.
- **Activities:** Reading texts with CVC words, searching for CVC patterns, writing rhyming CVC words.
- **Contribution to Goals:** Establishes the basics of decoding simple words, essential for early reading development.

Week 2: Exploring Silent E Words (Volume 2)

- **Focus:** Understanding the role of silent 'e' in changing the vowel sound to make it long.
- **Activities:** Identifying silent 'e' in texts, converting CVC words to CVCe words.
- **Contribution to Goals:** Enhances ability to decode and comprehend words with silent 'e', a crucial step in advancing reading skills.

Week 3: Delving into Digraphs and "Tch" (Volume 3)

- **Focus:** "Th," "sh," "ph," "wh," "ch," "ck," "qu" digraphs, and "tch."
- **Activities:** "Search the digraph in the given texts," creating lists of words for each digraph.
- **Contribution to Goals:** Expands vocabulary by introducing complex sounds, improving phonemic awareness and decoding skills.

Week 4: Blends and "Nk," "Ng" Blends (Volume 4)

- **Focus:** L, R, S, T blends and "nk," "ng" blends.
- **Activities:** Reading passages containing blends, identifying and writing words with blends.
- **Contribution to Goals:** Strengthens fluency by mastering blends, aiding in smoother reading of words and sentences.

Week 5: Vowel Teams (Volume 5)

- **Focus:** Vowel teams "ai," "ee," "ie," "oa."
- **Activities:** "Answer the questions" based on texts with vowel teams, finding and underlining vowel teams in sentences.
- **Contribution to Goals:** Improves understanding of vowel sounds and their variations, enhancing decoding of complex words.

Week 6: Advanced Phonics Concepts (Volume 6)

- **Focus:** Bossy "R," "y" as a vowel, "ow" as long o, ou, ow, oi, and short "oo."
- **Activities:** Exercises include rewriting sentences to include words with these phonics rules, "write the rhyming words for the words given."
- **Contribution to Goals:** Deepens phonics knowledge, broadening reading and spelling skills with more challenging phonetic patterns.

Week 7: The /oo/ Sound Variations (Volume 7)

- **Focus:** /oo/ sound as in "oo," "UI," "ew," "ue," "u_e," "igh."
- **Activities:** Activities like "search the text for /oo/ sound variations," creating sentences with /oo/ sound words.
- **Contribution to Goals:** Enhances ability to recognize and use varied vowel sounds, supporting advanced reading proficiency.

–

Week 8: Complex Phonics Patterns (Volume 8)

- **Focus:** "Au," "aw," soft c, soft g, fszl rule.
- **Activities:** Comprehensive review exercises, "rewrite the sentences" with focus words, engaging in creative writing using learned phonics patterns.
- **Contribution to Goals:** Consolidates all learned phonics concepts, ensuring a thorough understanding and application in reading and writing, preparing learners for continued reading success beyond the program.

Each week's plan is thoughtfully designed to contribute to the overarching goal of improving reading abilities through a gradual, cumulative learning process. By progressing through these volumes, learners will develop a robust foundation in phonics, significantly enhancing their decoding skills, reading fluency, comprehension, and overall confidence in reading.

TO SUM UP

As we stand at the threshold of a journey that promises to transform the way you or your loved ones engage with reading, it's time to take that decisive step forward. "The 8 Week Orton-Gillingham Decodable Readers Plan" is more than just a guide; it's your companion on a path to unlocking the full potential of reading proficiency. This is an invitation to commit to a plan that has been meticulously designed to address and overcome reading difficulties, ensuring a future where reading is not a challenge but a joy.

We understand the hurdles that come with dyslexia and other reading challenges—the frustration, the setbacks, and the moments of doubt. However, within these pages lies a structured, empathetic approach that speaks to the heart of these difficulties. By embarking on this 8-week journey, you are not just investing in a book; you are opening the door to a world where words flow with ease, where stories come alive, and where information becomes accessible.

Take the First Step:

Commit to dedicating a few moments each day to follow the plan laid out in this book. With each week's progression, you will witness firsthand the transformative power of dedicated practice, guided by the principles of the Orton-Gillingham approach. This isn't merely about learning to read—it's about gaining the confidence to explore, learn, and grow through the written word.

Expect Positive Change:

Change is a process, and with each step of this program, you'll see evidence of improvement. Whether it's for yourself, your child, or your students, expect to see a blossoming of reading skills, a boost in confidence, and an awakening of a love for reading. These aren't just goals; they are the outcomes that countless individuals have experienced through the dedication to this method.

You Are Supported:

Remember, you are not alone on this journey. This book serves as your roadmap, filled with activities, strategies, and encouragement designed to guide you through every challenge and celebrate every victory. Beyond these pages lies a community of educators, parents, and learners who share your aspirations and challenges. Together, there is no limit to what can be achieved.

Embrace the Journey:

Now is the moment to embrace this opportunity, to turn the page on reading difficulties, and to start a new chapter filled with success and growth. Let "The 8 Week Orton-Gillingham Decodable Readers Plan" be the catalyst for change, guiding you or your loved ones to become proficient, confident readers.

The journey to transformative reading starts here—commit to the path, engage with each week's plan, and watch as the world of reading opens up like never before. Welcome to the beginning of a life-changing experience.

Table of Contents

'L' blends

(bl words) Ava's Inspiration	(cl words) Pattrick the Clown	(fl words) The Dancing Flamingo	(gl words) Traveler of the Gleam Land	(pl words) The Plum Trees

Activities

Rhyming words	Questions and Answers	Story Reading	Find the Words
Pictures names	Matching Activity	Coloring Activity	Drawing Activity

Target Words

Blind black blue blink blender blade blank blow blazer blessed clever clown clay clam clock clue clenched click clapped flamingo flowers flag fluttered flood flow flapped flowing flakes flames gleam glaciers glass glow glory globe glowed gloves glittering glasses glue plot plum plan plant planting playing plucking pliers plug

Ava's Inspiration

Ava was a blind artist; she worked on her masterpiece using shades of blue and black. One day, while she was thinking about her next project, a sudden blink of inspiration caught her attention. She mixed the paints in the blender and started working on a blank canvas. She applied the paint onto the canvas with a blade, and with a swift blow of her breath, the painting came to life. She painted skyscrapers under the night light. A man in a blazer was standing under the shade of the lamp. She felt blessed to work on her inspiration.

Ava's Inspiration

Read the story and write all the 'bl' words found in the story.

Write the rhyming words for the words given below.

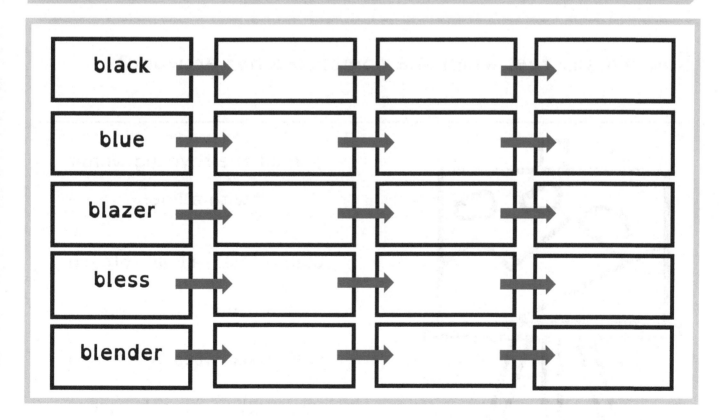

Ava's Inspiration

Who was Ava?

_____

How did Ava mix the colors?

_____

What did Ava paint?

_____

What did she use to apply the paint on the canvas?

_____

How did she feel when she completed her artwork?

_____

Join all the rhyming words
with a line.

blue   black   blow   bleach

back   flu   low   reach

clue   hack   teach   throw

rack   glue   preach   crow

4

Trace:

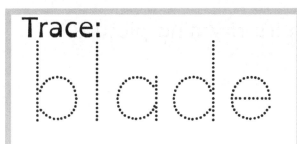

Say the word 3 times.

(1) (2) (3)

Draw a blade.

Find the 'bl' words.

b	l	o	o	d	s	b
l	h	i	c	k	s	l
a	o	e	r	n	e	a
d	b	l	u	e	l	c
e	r	a	m	e	b	k

Write the names of the pictures given below.

Rhymes with	Begins with
Razor	Bl_____
Docks	Bl_____
Flow	Bl_____
Clue	Bl_____
Rack	Bl_____
Fade	Bl_____

Patrick the Clown

Once upon a time, there lived a clever clown named Patrick, who loved to make kids laugh with his jokes and magic tricks. One day, he invited kids over to play with clay. The kids were sculpting and molding the clay, and a kid named Ronald made a clam out of the clay. Another kid made a clay clock, while others still did not have a clue what to make. A small girl seemed worried and clenched her fists repeatedly, as she was confused about what to make. Patrick gave the little girl a box, and she opened it with a faint click. Inside was a small pearl. The girl gave it a thought and in no time made a clay necklace. Everyone clapped for her, and she felt accomplished on her masterpiece.

Patrick the Clown

Read the story and write all the 'cl' words found in the story.

Write the rhyming words for the words given below.

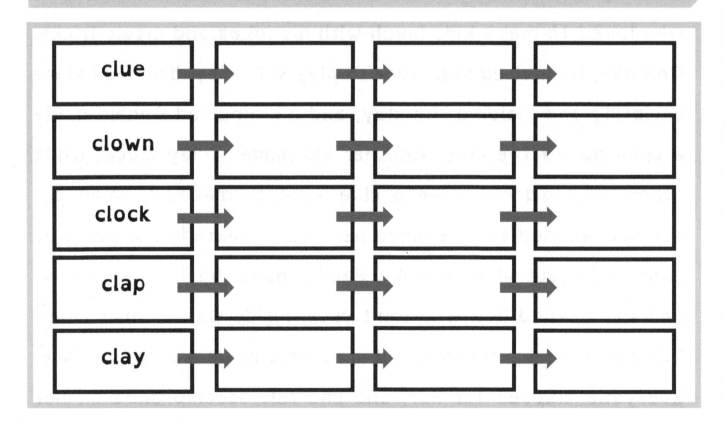

8

Patrick the Clown

Who was Patrick?

_____

What did Patrick love to do?

_____

Whom did Patrick invite and why?

_____

What did Ronald make?

_____

Why was the small girl worried?

_____

Join all the rhyming words
with a line.

clue   clock   clay   clan

block   flu   plan   reach

blue   rock   man   hay

dock   glue   ray   fan

9

Trace:

clown

Say the word 3 times.

(1) (2) (3)

Draw a clown.

Find the 'cl' words.

c	l	a	p	d	s	b
l	l	i	c	k	s	n
o	o	i	r	n	e	a
w	b	l	c	e	l	l
n	r	a	m	K	b	c

Write the names of the pictures given below.

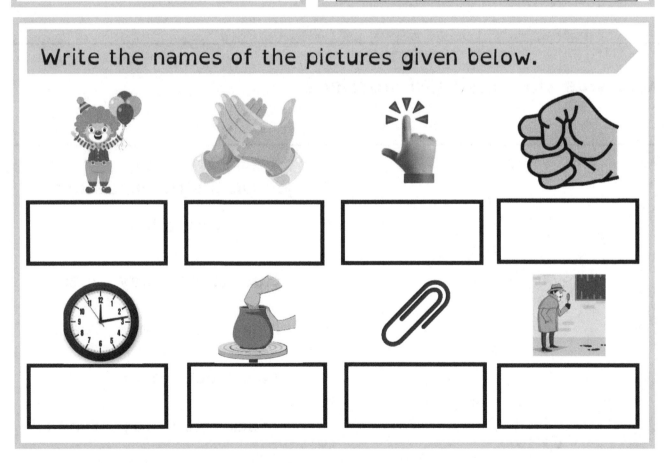

Rhymes with	Begins with
Block	Cl_____
Flip	Cl_____
Drench	Cl_____
Flap	Cl_____
Flick	Cl_____
Town	Cl_____

The Dancing Flamingo

Fiona was a graceful flamingo who loved to dance among the flowers in the middle of the beautiful meadow. While Fiona was dancing to the breeze of wind, a flag fluttered near the fence. Fiona heard a loud noise and the trees started shaking. She looked back and was in shock to see a flood was coming her way. The flow of the water was very fast. Fiona flapped her wings and tried to fly away. Fiona flew above the rising waters. Fiona looked at the stream of water which was flowing with the petals of flowers, broken branches, and flakes of sunlight. Fiona saw flames coming from a distant campfire, she knew that it must be safe for her to land there. She flapped her wings and landed to the safe ground.

The Dancing Flamingo

Write the rhyming words for the words given below.

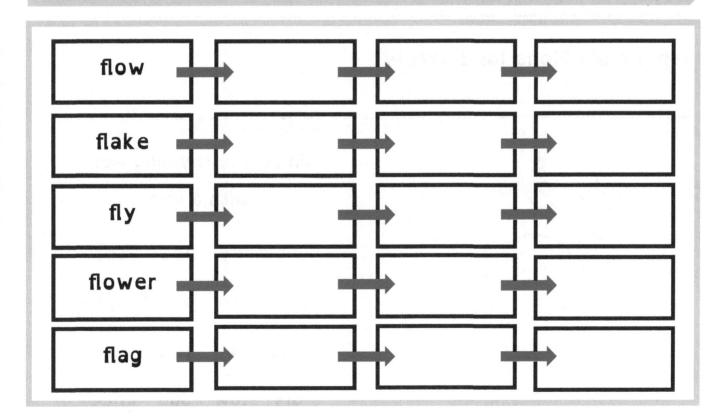

flow →

flake →

fly →

flower →

flag →

13

The Dancing Flamingo

Who was Fiona?

_____

What did Fiona love to do?

_____

What happened when Fiona was dancing?

_____

How did Fiona save herself from the flood?

_____

Where did Fiona land safely?

_____

Join all the rhyming words with a line.
flow   fly   flea   flood
my   blow   blood   plea
crow   by   bud   hay
dry   slow   dud   knee

Trace:	Say the word 3 times.

Trace:

flower

Say the word 3 times.

(1)   (2)   (3)

Draw a flower.

Find the 'fl' words.

f	l	o	w	e	r	f
l	l	i	c	k	s	l
o	f	l	o	o	d	y
w	b	l	c	e	l	l
f	l	a	m	e	b	c

Write the names of the pictures given below.

Rhymes with	Begins with
Plea	Fl_____
Ply	Fl_____
Task	Fl_____
Rake	Fl_____
Tower	Fl_____
Rag	Fl_____

Traveler of the Gleam Land

Gleam Land was a small town in the middle of the glaciers. The glaciers shimmered like glass under the glow of the sun. A resident of the town was a traveler, so he embarked on a journey to look for glory. He had a magical globe in his bag that glowed when going towards the right path. The traveler put on his gloves and started his journey. On his way, he encountered mighty glaciers, the lands covered in glass ice, and the trees filled with glittering snow. The traveler's glasses broke while he was walking on the glass ice. He mended his glasses with the glue. He continued his journey to look for glory.

Traveler of the Gleam Land

Write the rhyming words for the words given below.

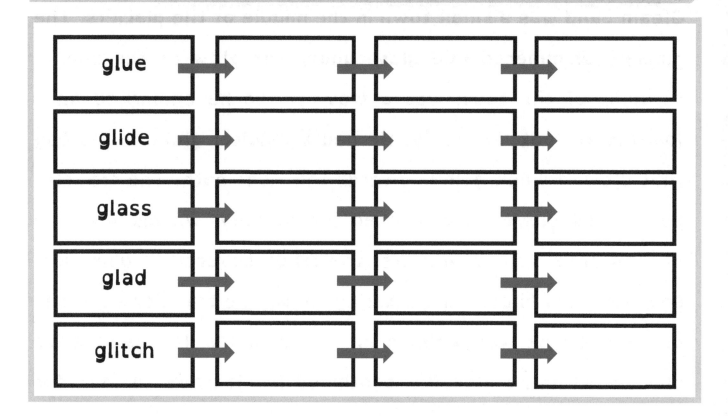

Traveler of the Gleam Land

What was the name of the town?

_____

Where was the town situated?

_____

Why did the traveler set on a journey?

_____

What did he take with him?

_____

How did he fix his broken glasses?

_____

Join all the rhyming words with a line.
glow   glass   glide   glue
brass   blow   slide   flu
crow   mass   hide   true
class   slow   sue   ride

Trace:

glass

Say the word 3 times.

(1) (2) (3)

Draw a glass.

Find the 'gl' words.

g	l	o	g	e	r	g
l	l	i	l	k	d	l
e	f	l	o	o	a	a
e	b	l	w	e	l	s
g	l	a	m	e	g	s

Write the names of the pictures given below.

Write the word and match it with its rhyming picture.

Rhymes with	Begins with
Bad	Gl_____
Brass	Gl_____
Blue	Gl_____
Floss	Gl_____
Heater	Gl_____
Dove	Gl_____

The Plum Trees

Jack was a farmer; he had a small plot of land. He had planted plum trees on the plot. One day, he had a plan in mind and carefully looked for the perfect spot to plant the sapling. While he was planting, he heard a playful laughter. Upon investigating, he found out that a few kids were playing under a plum tree; they were plucking the fruit off its branches. Jack felt energetic to see the little kids playing. He grabbed the pliers, a basket, and a plug to harvest some plums. He realized that happiness comes from spontaneous moments of joy.

The Plum Trees

Read the story and write all the 'pl' words found in the story.

Write the rhyming words for the words given below.

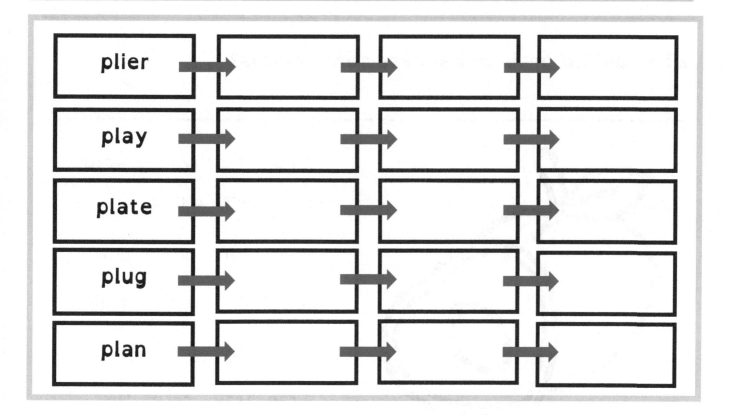

The Plum Trees

What was the name of the man?

_____

What had Jack planted on his plot?

_____

What plan did Jack have in mind?

_____

What were the kids doing?

_____

What did he grab to harvest some plums?

_____

Join all the rhyming words
with a line.

play   plan   plier   plate

man   hay   mate   higher

tan   bay   fire   hate

ran   tray   rate   tire

Trace:

plum

Say the word 3 times.

(1)   (2)   (3)

Draw a plum.

Find the 'pl' words.

p	l	o	t	e	n	p
l	l	i	l	k	a	l
p	l	e	a	o	l	
e	b	l	w	e	p	t
p	l	a	y	e	g	e

Write the names of the pictures given below.

Write the word and match it with its rhyming picture.

Rhymes with	Begins with
Slug	Pl_____
Late	Pl_____
Slum	Pl_____
Clay	Pl_____
Slot	Pl_____
Higher	Pl_____

'R' blends

(gr words)	(pr words)	(cr words)	(dr words)	(fr words)
The Groom's Party	The Grand Prize	The Curse of the Prince	The Golden Egg	Pamela and the Frog

(br words)	(tr words)
The Trail of Thoughts	Trevor's Trolley

Activities

Rhyming words	Questions and Answers	Story Reading	Find the Words
Pictures names	Matching Activity	Coloring Activity	Drawing Activity

Target Words

Greg   green   groom   grill   grass   grilled   grape   grain   gravy   grasshopper   gracious   pram   pretty   present   pretzel   prize   printed   printer   prick   cripple   crow   crab   crying   creature   cracked   dragons   dragonflies   drake   drowned   draw   dream   dress   drape   dripping   frilly   frock   frame   friend   frog   grapevine   freed   frozen   French   fries   Fred   brown   bridge   break   bread   broom   bride   broken   branches   Trevor   trolley   trash   truck   tractor   trumpet   trembling   tree   treasure

The Groom's Party

Greg lived in a beautiful house which was surrounded by lush green gardens. Greg was a newly wedded groom and was hosting a party in honor of his new bride. He had set up a grill on the green grass. The perfect grid marks were left on the marinated grilled meat once it was done. The guests were welcomed with grape juice. The guests were in awe looking at the golden grain fields. The guests were served with freshly made gravy along with the grilled meat. Greg noticed a small grasshopper hopping on the grass. Greg gave a gracious toast to his bride and guests.

The Groom's Party

Read the story and write all the 'gr' words found in the story.

Write the rhyming words for the words given below.

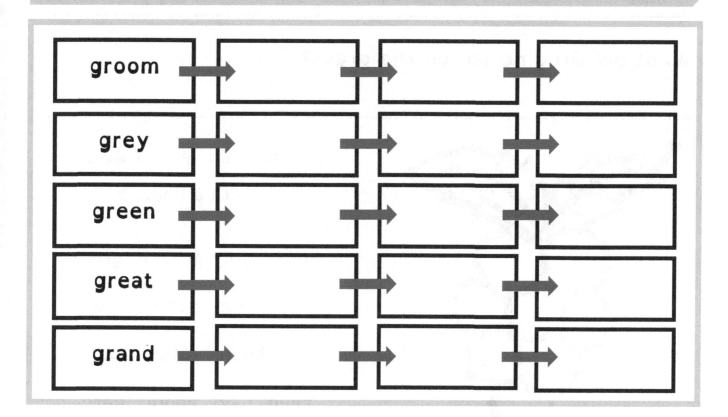

The Groom's Party

What was Greg's house surrounded with?

_____

Why was Greg hosting the party?

_____

What was on the menu?

_____

What were the guests welcomed with?

_____

What did Greg notice on the grass?

_____

Join all the rhyming words with a line.

Green   grey   groom   great

day   lean   doom   bait

hay   been   fate   zoom

seen   bay   boom   hate

Trace:
grapes

Say the word 3 times.
1   2   3

Draw three grapes.

Find the 'gr' words.

b	g	r	i	l	l	g
g	r	a	p	e	s	r
a	o	e	r	n	e	e
d	b	l	u	e	l	e
g	r	e	y	e	b	n

Write the names of the pictures given below.

Rhymes with	Begins with
Drapes	Gr_____
Brain	Gr_____
Pray	Gr_____
Seen	Gr_____
Drill	Gr_____
Brass	Gr_____

The Grand Prize

Once upon a morning in a busy town, a mother struggled to push her pretty pram by the sidewalk. Her baby was sleeping inside the pram. She stopped at a gift shop to buy a present for her baby. She looked at all the options and bought a soft plush toy and a tiny pretzel. As she was about to leave the shop, the shop owner stopped her and gave her an offer: she could win a prize if she would tell him her name. The woman told the owner of the shop her name. He printed her name on a small sheet of paper from an old printer machine. A week later, when the announcements were made, she looked at the ticket, and a prick of excitement ran through her. She was the winner of the grand prize. She embraced her little one in excitement, knowing that with the grand prize money, she could give her child a beautiful life.

The Grand Prize

Read the story and write all the 'pr' words found in the story.

Make sentences using the following words.

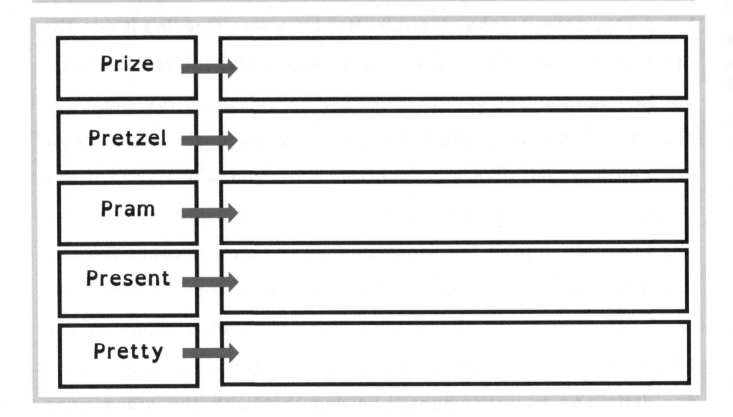

Prize	
Pretzel	
Pram	
Present	
Pretty	

The Grand Prize

What was the woman struggling with?

_____

Who was inside the pram?

_____

Why did the woman go inside the shop?

_____

What did the woman buy?

_____

How did the woman win the grand prize?

_____

Join all the rhyming words
with a line.

pram   pretty   prize   pret

pity   tram   let   size

ham   kitty   met   lies

city   dam   set   cries

35

Trace:

pram

Say the word 3 times.

(1) (2) (3)

Draw a pram.

Find the 'pr' words.

p	r	e	a	c	h	p
p	r	i	d	e	s	r
a	o	e	r	n	e	a
d	p	r	o	u	d	m
p	r	e	s	e	n	t

Write the names of the pictures given below.

Rhymes with	Begins with
Splint	Pr_____
Fiest	Pr_____
Slam	Pr_____
Trick	Pr_____
Fries	Pr_____
Finse	Pr_____

The Curse of the Prince

Once upon a time, a prince who lived in the forest was transformed into a cripple because of an ancient curse. He only had one friend in the forest, which was a crow. The prince would send the crow daily in search of a way to break his curse. One day, the crow was perched atop a tree when he saw a crab pulling a small chest covered in chains. The crow flew towards the crab, the crab started crying looking at the majestic crow flying towards the tiny creature. The crab ran away and left the chest behind. The crow took the chest to the prince. The prince cracked open the chains of the chest. Inside was a magical potion that would transform the prince back into his old self. The prince drank the potion and danced gleefully to the tunes of nature.

The Curse of the Prince

Read the story and write all the 'cr' words found in the story.

Make sentences using the following words.

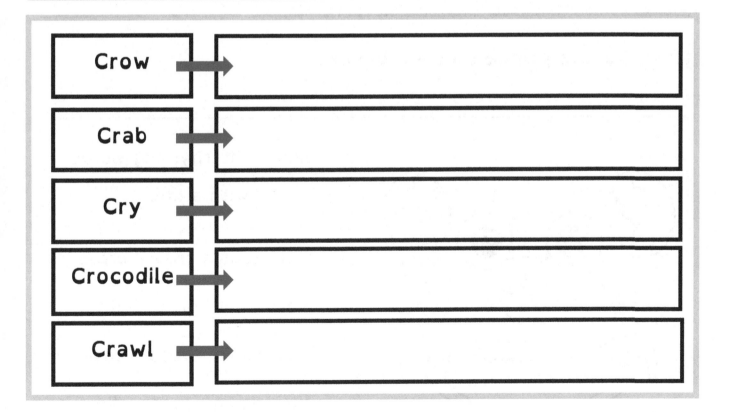

Crow	
Crab	
Cry	
Crocodile	
Crawl	

The Curse of the Prince

Where did the prince live?

_____

What was the curse of the prince?

_____

Who was the prince's friend?

_____

What did the crow see from the tree?

_____

How did the prince's curse break?

_____

Join all the rhyming words with a line.

crab crown crow   cross

frown cab grow   floss

lab town boss   low

city down moss   flow

Trace:

crab

Say the word 3 times.

(1) (2) (3)

Draw a crab.

Find the 'cr' words.

c	r	a	b	c	h	c
c	r	a	c	k	s	r
c	r	o	w	n	e	o
d	c	r	a	n	e	w
p	c	r	a	s	h	t

Write the names of the pictures given below.

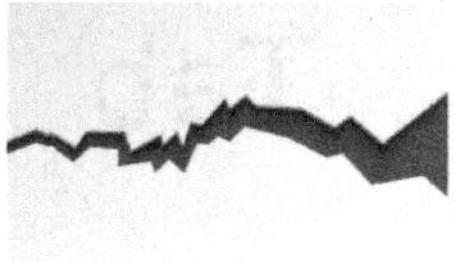

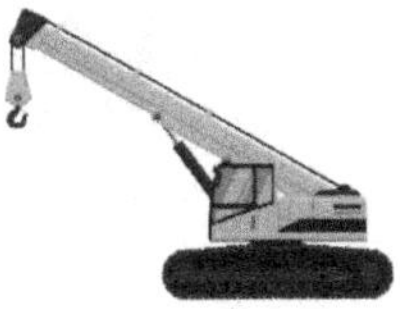

Write the word and match it with its rhyming picture.

Rhymes with	Begins with
Try	Cr_____
Main	Cr_____
Town	Cr_____
Tab	Cr_____
Flow	Cr_____
Track	Cr_____

The Golden Egg

Lyla lived on the land of dragons. She loved watching the dragonflies dance till sunset. One day, while she was feeding her dragon, a drake came to Lyla and asked for her help. He told Lyla that his golden egg had drowned in the depths of the lake. Lyla asked the drake to draw his golden egg on a sheet of paper so that she could help him find his egg. Lyla wore her dream dress and asked her dragon to go into the depths of water and look for the drake's egg. The dragon dived into the water and looked through every single drape. Finally, he came out dripping in water with the golden egg. Lyla handed over the egg to the drake.

The Golden Egg

Read the story and write all the 'dr' words found in the story.

Make sentences using the following words.

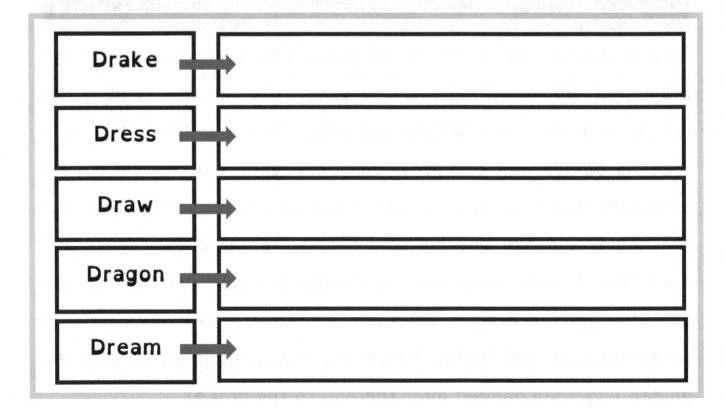

Drake	→	
Dress	→	
Draw	→	
Dragon	→	
Dream	→	

The Golden Egg

What is the name of the girl?

_____

On which land did Lyla live?

_____

What was the drake's problem?

_____

What did the drake draw on the paper?

_____

How did the dragon help Lyla?

_____

Join all the rhyming words with a line.

drake	dream	dress	cry
beam	break	try	press
take	seem	fry	mess
team	lake	my	chess

45

Trace:

dress

Say the word 3 times.

(1) (2) (3)

Draw a dress.

Find the 'dr' words.

e	r	a	b	c	h	d
k	r	a	c	k	s	r
a	r	d	r	i	p	e
r	d	r	a	w	e	s
d	r	a	g	o	n	s

Write the names of the pictures given below.

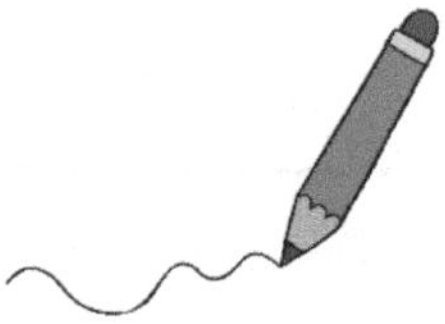

Rhymes with	Begins with
Grill	Dr_____
Shrink	Dr_____
Plum	Dr_____
Press	Dr_____
Straw	Dr_____
Strive	Dr_____

Pamela and the Frog

Pamela wore her favorite red frilly frock. She kept a tiny frame inside her backpack and skipped towards the pond, where her friend Fred the frog was waiting for her. On the way to the pond, her shoe got stuck in the grapevine. She freed herself from the grapevine and went on her way. As she reached the pond, she took out the frame and gave it to Fred. Fred croaked and said thank you. The lake was frozen due to the cold, and Fred couldn't swim anymore. Pamela offered French fries to Fred. They both shared the meal sitting beside the frozen pond.

Pamela and the Frog

Read the story and write all the 'fr' words found in the story.

Make sentences using the following words.

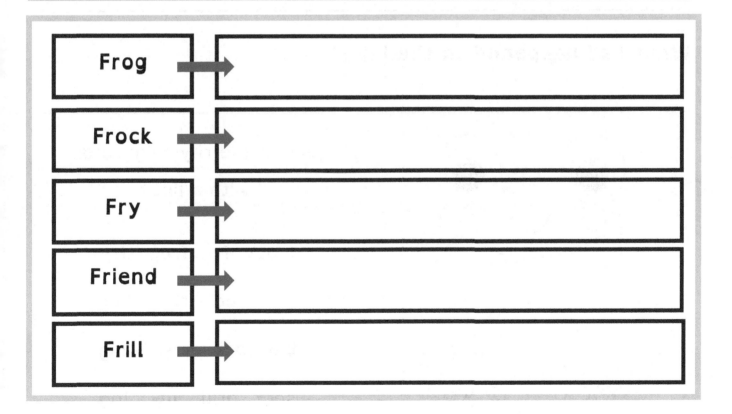

Frog	
Frock	
Fry	
Friend	
Frill	

Pamela and the Frog

What is the name of the girl?

_____

Who was the girl's best friend?

_____

What was the girl wearing?

_____

What was inside her backpack?

_____

What had happened to the lake?

_____

Join all the rhyming words
with a line.

frock frill frog fry

drill rock try hog

bill lock cry dog

sock grill my log

50

Trace:

frock

Say the word 3 times.

(1) (2) (3)

Draw a frock.

Find the 'fr' words.

f	r	i	e	n	d	f
r	r	a	c	k	s	r
i	r	y	r	i	p	o
l	f	r	e	e	e	c
l	r	a	g	o	n	k

Write the names of the pictures given below.

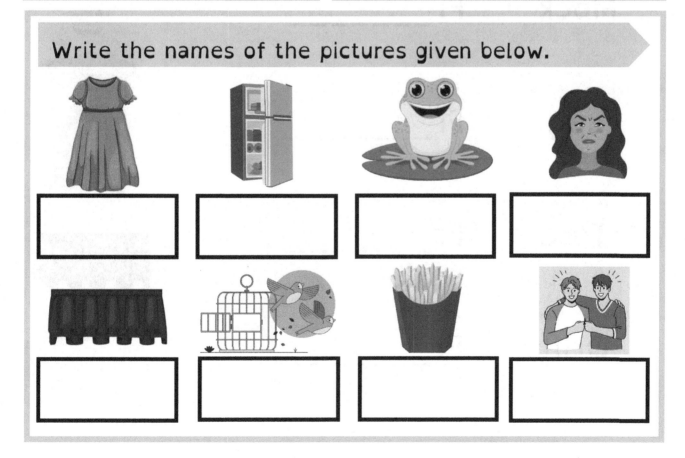

Rhymes with	Begins with
Bridge	Fr_____
Brown	Fr_____
Mock	Fr_____
Log	Fr_____
Tree	Fr_____
Drill	Fr_____

The Trail of Thoughts

A man in a brown jacket was walking on a bridge, his brain filled with thoughts and worries. His face could tell that he was worried. He wanted to break free of all the thoughts. His trail of thoughts broke free with the smell of freshly baked bread from a bakery. He felt compelled to follow the fragrance. He went inside; the baker was sweeping the floor with a broom. The baker welcomed him and offered him freshly baked bread and a cup of coffee. The man took a sip and looked outside the window. A bride was smiling, holding a yellow bouquet. The man suddenly felt fresh and at ease. The baker sat with him and shared his story of love and loss. The man decided to mend the broken branches of his past and moved on with a smile on his face.

The Trail of Thoughts

Read the story and write all the 'br' words found in the story.

Make sentences using the following words.

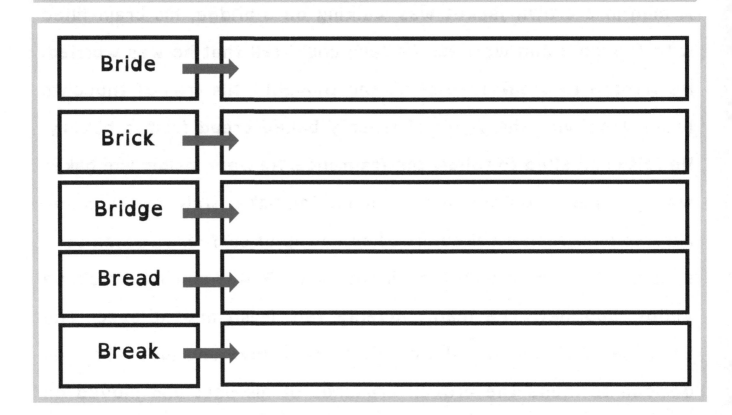

Bride	
Brick	
Bridge	
Bread	
Break	

The Trail of Thoughts

Where was the man walking?

_____

What was the man thinking?

_____

What did the man see outside the window?

_____

What was the baker doing?

_____

What compelled the man to break free of his thoughts?

_____

Join all the rhyming words
with a line.

frock frill frog   fry

drill rock   try   hog

bill   lock   cry   dog

sock grill   my   log

55

Trace:

bridge

Say the word 3 times.

(1) (2) (3)

Draw a bridge.

Find the 'br' words.

m	r	i	e	n	d	e
o	b	r	a	i	n	d
o	r	y	r	i	p	i
r	b	r	e	a	d	r
b	r	i	d	g	e	b

Write the names of the pictures given below.

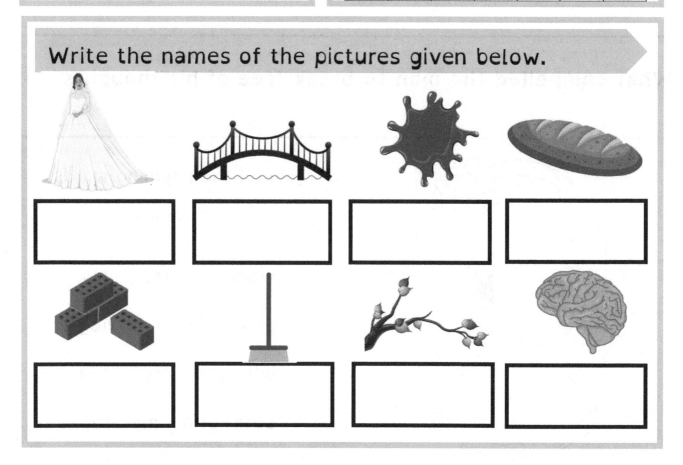

Write the word and match it with its rhyming picture.

Rhymes with	Begins with
Room	Br_____
Trick	Br_____
Ranch	Br_____
Lead	Br_____
Town	Br_____
Train	Br_____

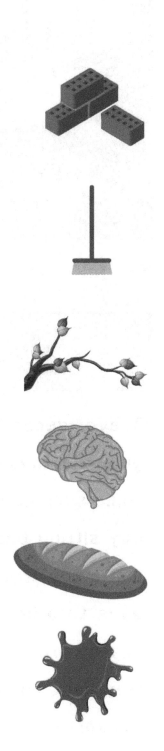

Trevor's Trolley

Trevor decorated all his toys on a trolley and set on a mission to give the toys to needy children. He was looking for the children while walking in the streets of the town for hours. He saw a little boy sitting beside a trash can. Trevor went to the boy and gave him a toy truck. The tractor was Trevor's favorite toy, which he gave to a little girl who was sweeping the streets. He went to a nearby orphanage and gave his trumpet to a trembling boy. On the way back home, he sat under an apple tree and ate a fallen fruit. Trevor knew that not even the greatest treasure could grant Trevor the feeling of accomplishment he had right now.

Trevor's Trolley

Read the story and write all the 'tr' words found in the story.

Make sentences using the following words.

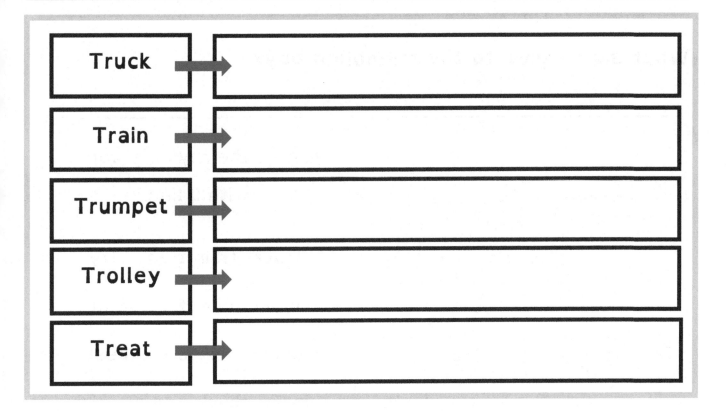

Truck

Train

Trumpet

Trolley

Treat

The Trail of Thoughts

What is the name of the boy in the story?

_____

What was inside Trevor's trolley?

_____

Who did Trevor give the truck to?

_____

To whom did Trevor give the tractor?

_____

What did he give to the trembling boy?

_____

Join all the rhyming words
with a line.

truck   train treat   try

brain luck   fry   feat

buck   rain   cry   beat

main   chuck   meet   lie

60

Trace:

truck

Say the word 3 times.

(1) (2) (3)

Draw a truck.

Find the 'tr' words.

t	r	a	i	n	d	t
r	b	r	y	i	n	r
u	r	r	r	i	p	e
c	t	r	e	a	d	e
k	t	r	a	d	e	b

Write the names of the pictures given below.

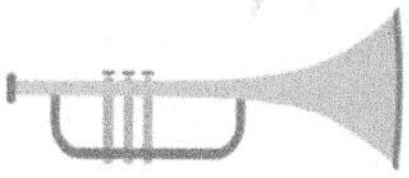

Rhymes with	Begins with
Puppet	Tr_____
Luck	Tr_____
Free	Tr_____
Brain	Tr_____
Bash	Tr_____
Actor	Tr_____

'S' blends

(sk/sc words)	(sp words)	(st words)	(sl words)	(sm words)
The Abandoned Mansion	The Enchantress	Stella's Dream	The Slimy Slug	Mia and the Smuggler

Activities

Rhyming words	Questions and Answers	Story Reading	Find the Words
Pictures names	Matching Activity	Coloring Activity	Drawing Activity

Target Words

Skirt   school   scooter   sky   screwdriver   skunk   scream   screen
skeleton   skull   spell   spoon   speak   spin   spade   spider   spied
spirit   Stella   stepmother   steel   stairs   stage   stand   stove   stormy
steal   slug   slimy   slide   slope   slip   slippers   slice   slow   sleep
smile   smoothie   small   smirk   smuggler   smart

The Abandoned Mansion

Sally put on her skirt, wore her uniform, and got ready for an adventurous day at school. Sally started her scooter and reached the school under the beautiful sky. After school, Sally and her friends decided to explore an abandoned mansion behind the school. Sally opened the door with a screwdriver and went inside. As they all stepped inside the house, a strange smell came. They were startled to see a skunk sleeping in the room. Sally's scream woke up the skunk. The skunk ran and hid behind the TV screen. One of Sally's friend bumped into a skeleton and the skull fell. All the girls screamed in fear and ran outside the mansion. Sally decided never to go into any strange place alone.

The Abandoned Mansion

Write the rhyming words for the words given below.

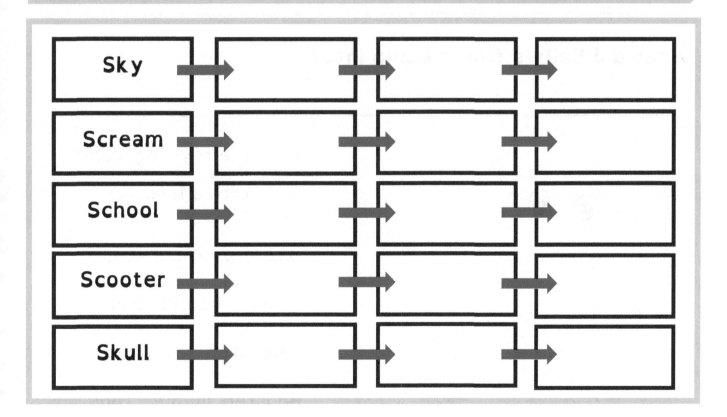

Sky			
Scream			
School			
Scooter			
Skull			

The Abandoned Mansion

Answer the questions asked below.

Where was Sally going?

_____

Where did Sally and her friends decide to go?

_____

How did Sally open the door?

_____

Why was the strange smell coming from the house?

_____

What did Sally's friend bump into?

_____

Join all the rhyming words with a line.

scooter   school   skull

pool   Hooter   dull

Rooster   fool   null

Booster   hurdle   tool

Trace:

skirt

Say the word 3 times.

(1) (2) (3)

Draw a skirt.

Find the 'sk/sc' words.

s	c	h	o	o	l	s
s	k	u	n	k	s	k
a	s	k	i	p	e	y
s	k	i	r	t	p	e
s	c	r	e	w	s	n

Write the names of the pictures given below.

Rhymes with	Begins with
Pool	Sc_____
Team	Sc_____
Dull	Sk_____
Trunk	Sk_____
Fly	Sk_____
Shirt	Sk_____

The Enchantress

Clara was an enchantress. She would use a silver spoon as a wand and weave the magical spells. Everyone came to her for the solution of their worries. Clara was tending to her garden with a silver spade when she heard whispers coming from the wind. Upon hearing closely, the winds spoke to her and asked her for help. The winds took a spin around Clara and vanished suddenly. Clara sped her way and reached the land of spiders. One spider told her that their village was possessed by an evil spirit. Clara cast a spell with her silver spoon, and in no time the evil spirit left the village.

The Enchantress

Write the rhyming words for the words given below.

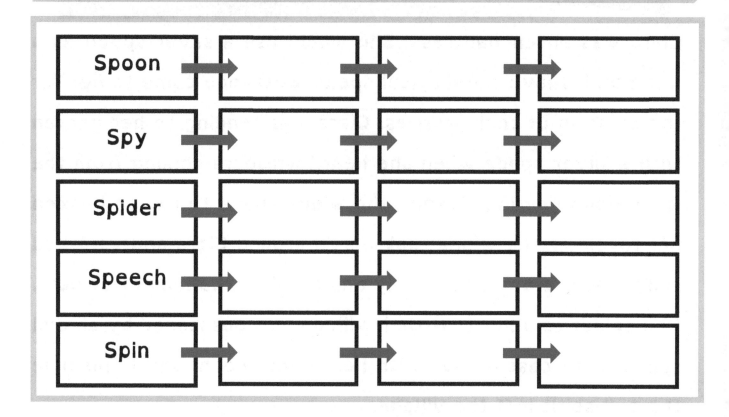

The Enchantress

What did Clara do?

_____

How did Clara use her magic spells?

_____

How did Clara help the spiders?

_____

Whose village was possessed?

_____

What was Clara doing when she heard the whispers?

_____

Join all the rhyming words
with a line.

Spell speech spin   speak

teach well   reek   tin

reach tell   leak   fin

beach bell   beak   bin

71

Trace:

spoon

Say the word 3 times.

(1)　(2)　(3)

Draw a spoon.

Find the 'sp words.

s	p	i	n	o	s	s
w	k	u	n	k	p	p
s	p	i	l	l	i	o
o	k	f	r	t	t	o
s	p	e	a	k	g	n

Write the names of the pictures given below.

Rhymes with	Begins with
Fill	Sp_____
Win	Sp_____
Arrow	Sp_____
Tear	Sp_____
Icy	Sp_____
Tell	Sp_____

Stella's Dream

Stella lived in a small town with her stepmother. Her stepmother would make Stella wash all the steel pots and scrub the floor and stairs daily. Stella had a magical voice; she would only dream of performing on the big stage. One story night, Stella took a big step of courage and went to the local theatre, where everyone was invited to perform on the big stage. Stella passed by a restaurant where a man was standing beside the stove. Stella entered the theatre and saw a big statue of a woman. When she stood on the stage, she was in shock to see so many people, but she took a deep breath and enchanted everyone with her magical voice and stole the show.

Stella's Dream

Read the story and write all the 'st' words found in the story.

Write the rhyming words for the words given below.

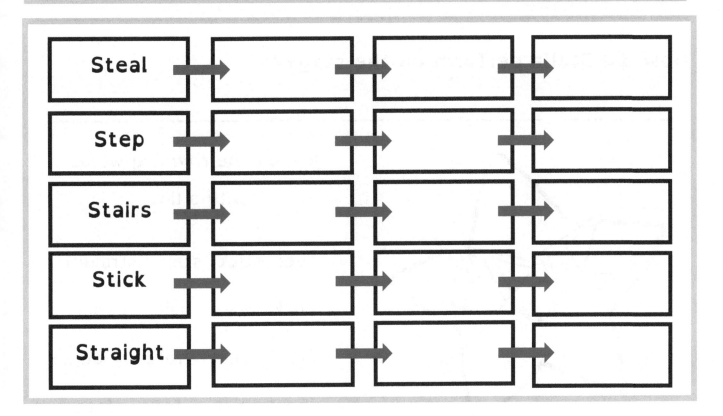

Steal	→		→		→	
Step	→		→		→	
Stairs	→		→		→	
Stick	→		→		→	
Straight	→		→		→	

Stella's Dream

Whom did Stella live with?

_____

What was Stella's daily routine?

_____

What was Stella's dream?

_____

What did Stella see on the way to the theatre?

_____

How did Stella perform on the stage?

_____

Join all the rhyming words
with a line.

steel   stick   stair   straight

lick   reel   bait   bear

flick   feel   rate   deer

heal   tick   fear   fate

76

Trace:

star

Say the word 3 times.

(1)　(2)　(3)

Draw a star.

Find the 'st' words.

s	t	o	r	y	s	s
t	t	u	n	k	t	t
a	p	e	l	l	e	i
n	k	f	p	t	e	c
d	p	e	a	k	l	k

Write the names of the pictures given below.

Rhymes with	Begins with
Norm	St_____
Car	St_____
Band	St_____
Lick	St_____
Meal	St_____
bear	St_____

The Slimy Slug

Once upon a time, there lived a slimy slug named Sammy, in a sleepy town. The slug loved to slide down the hill. One day, while he was sliding down the slide, his slippers got stuck in the moss. He tried to take out the slippers slowly. As soon as he freed himself from the moss, he slipped on the slab and fell. He fainted for a while, and when he opened his eyes, he found himself in an underground burrow that was filled with slices of cakes and pizzas. He feasted on the cake and pizza and fell asleep like a baby.

The Slimy Slug

Read the story and write all the 'sl' words found in the story.

Write the rhyming words for the words given below.

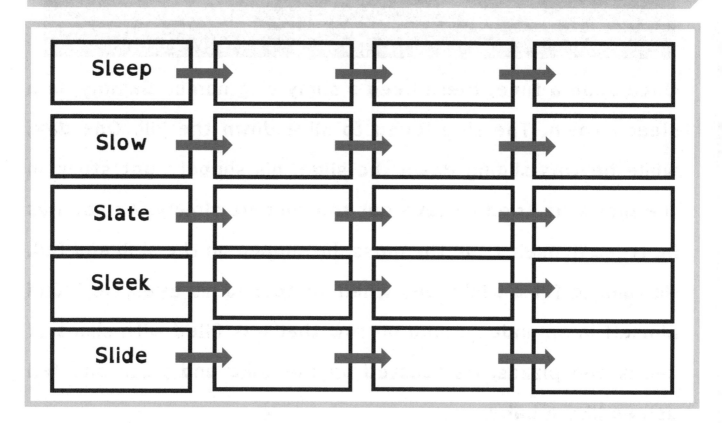

The Slimy Slug

Answer the questions asked below.

Where did the slug live?

_____

What did the slug love to do?

_____

What got stuck in the moss?

_____

What happened when he got himself free from the moss?

_____

What was inside the burrow?

_____

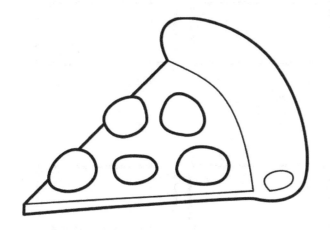

Join all the rhyming words
with a line.

slow   sleep   slate   slit

reap   blow   wit   bait

sheep   flow   bit   mate

plough   keep   fate   hit

81

Trace:

slug

Say the word 3 times.

(1) (2) (3)

Draw a slug.

Find the 'sl' words.

s	l	i	m	e	s	s
l	t	u	n	w	t	l
u	p	y	l	o	e	i
g	k	l	p	l	e	m
d	p	s	a	s	l	k

Write the names of the pictures given below.

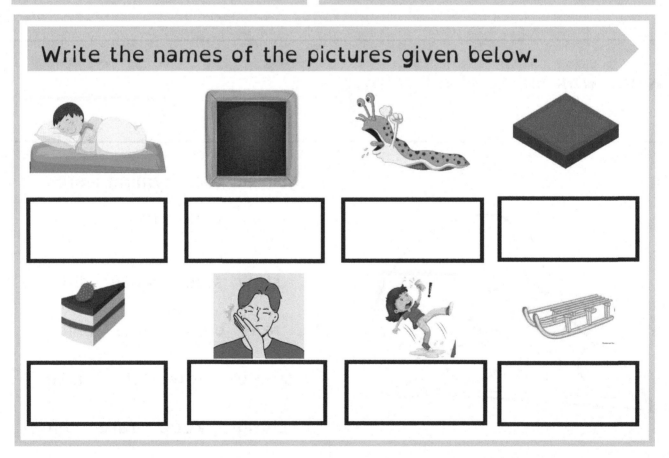

82

Write the word and match it with its rhyming picture.

Rhymes with	Begins with
Clap	Sl_____
Tab	Sl_____
Bled	Sl_____
Sheep	Sl_____
Clip	Sl_____
Late	Sl_____

Mia and the Smuggler

Mia was an owner of a small cafe. She was a smart barista. One day, she added random ingredients and made an unexpected smoothie. The taste of the smoothie was so good, that whoever tasted her smoothie couldn't stop smiling. One day, a smuggler came with a smirk on his face. Mia was smart, and she could smell something fishy. Mia gave a cup of hot chocolate to the smuggler, and she pressed the hidden red button that was under the counter so that local police could come. Mia sat with the smuggler and told him tales of her smoothie. The smuggler wanted to leave, but Mia kept him occupied with her tales. In no time, the police arrived and arrested the smuggler. The town was safe because of Mia's intelligence.

Mia and the Smuggler

Read the story and write all the 'sm' words found in the story.

Write the rhyming words for the words given below.

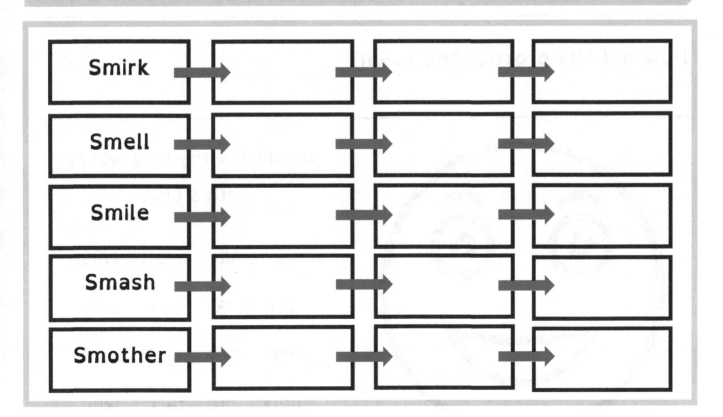

Smirk	→	→	→
Smell	→	→	→
Smile	→	→	→
Smash	→	→	→
Smother	→	→	→

Mia and the Smuggler

Who was Mia?

_____

What did Mia make?

_____

Who came to Mia's Café?

_____

How was Mia's smoothie and how did she make it?

_____

How did Mia protect the town?

_____

Join all the rhyming words
with a line.

smirk	smile	smell	smart
tile	lurk	bell	art
jerk	pile	cart	tell
perk	file	tart	well

Trace:

smile

Say the word 3 times.

(1) (2) (3)

Draw a smiling face.

Find the 'sm' words.

s	m	i	l	e	s	s
s	m	i	r	k	m	m
u	p	y	l	o	a	a
s	m	e	l	l	s	r
d	p	s	a	s	h	t

Write the names of the pictures given below.

Rhymes with	Begins with
Stall	Sm_____
Pile	Sm_____
Bash	Sm_____
Perk	Sm_____
Tell	Sm_____
Poke	Sm_____

'T' blends

(ct words) The Hidden Artifacts	(ft words) Kimberly's Raft	(lt words) Thomas and the Quilt	(nt words) The Traveler and the Saint	(pt words) The Struggling Playwright	(st words) The Archer's Tale

Activities

Rhyming words	Questions and Answers	Story Reading	Find the Words
Pictures names	Matching Activity	Coloring Activity	Drawing Activity

Target Words

Act   artifacts   collect   elect   pact   insect   inject   gift   soft

raft   lift   swift   quilt   built   knelt   guilt   felt   belt   halt

faint   paint   saint   tent   bent   panted   adapt   script   adopt   corrupt

kept   wept   crept   best   test   nest   guest   vest   rest   last   list

The Hidden Artifacts

Once upon a time in a forest, all the animals gathered to act upon an important issue. A few artifacts were scattered all around the jungle. They had to select a person to collect all the artifacts. The council held an election, and they all elected the fox, who was known for his bravery and cunningness. All the animals made a pact to help the fox. A little insect came with a magical ball and told the animals that if they injected the pond's water into it, the ball would glow and show the path to the hidden artifacts. All the animals gathered and followed the path led by the fox to help the jungle.

The Hidden Artifacts

Make sentences using the following words.

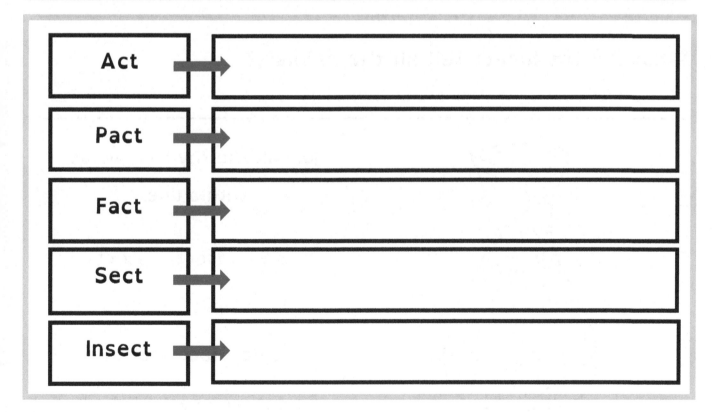

Act	
Pact	
Fact	
Sect	
Insect	

The Hidden Artifacts

Answer the questions asked below.

What did all the animals gather?

_____

Where did all the animals meet?

_____

What was the important matter?

_____

Who was elected for the matter?

_____

What did the insect tell all the animals?

_____

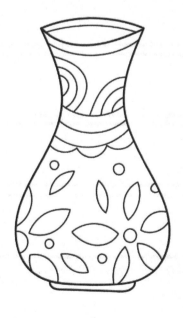

Join all the rhyming words with a line.

act   insect   strict

sect   pact   clicked

eject   fact   kicked

elect   compact   licked

92

Trace:

insect

Say the word 3 times.

(1) (2) (3)

Draw an insect.

Find the 'ct words.

i	n	s	e	c	t	s
s	e	l	e	c	t	t
a	s	k	i	p	e	c
f	a	c	t	g	p	a
s	c	r	e	w	s	p

Write the names of the pictures given below.

Rhymes with	Begins with
Affect	R_____
Sect	I_____
Aspect	I_____
Select	E_____
Pact	A_____
Fact	A_____

Kimberly's Raft

Kimberly was a little girl, who loved soft, plush toys. Her mother gifted her with a soft teddy bear. Kimberly loved it dearly. She loved doing some crafts. She made a raft and left it in the room. She brought her teddy and made him sit on the raft. She lifted the raft, took it outside, and put it inside the pool. With a swift blow of wind, the raft started moving. Kimberly played with her raft and the teddy for hours.

Kimberly's Raft

Make sentences using the following words.

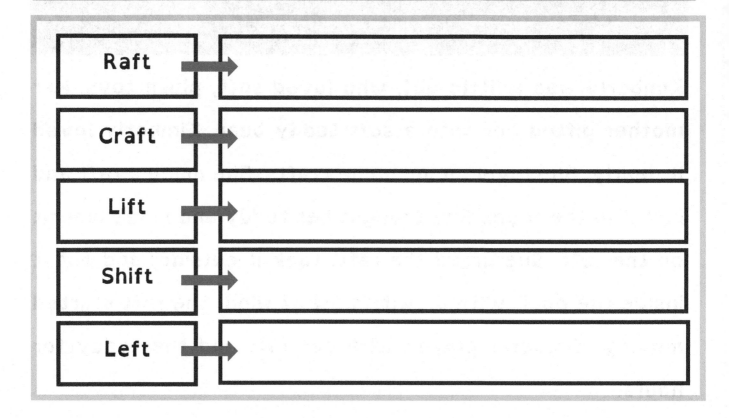

Raft

Craft

Lift

Shift

Left

Kimberly's Raft

What is the name of the girl in the story?

_____

What did the girl love the most?

_____

What did her mother gift her?

_____

What did the girl make?

_____

What did she do with the raft?

_____

Join all the rhyming words
with a line.

raft   lift   left

gift   craft   cleft

swift   theft   shaft

drift   compact   heft

97

Trace:

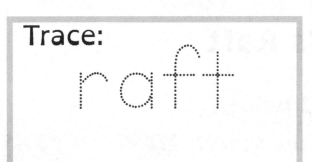

raft

Say the word 3 times.

(1) (2) (3)

Draw a raft.

Find the 'ft words.

c	r	a	f	t	t	r
s	w	i	f	t	f	a
l	e	f	t	p	a	f
f	a	c	t	g	h	t
s	c	r	e	w	s	p

Write the names of the pictures given below.

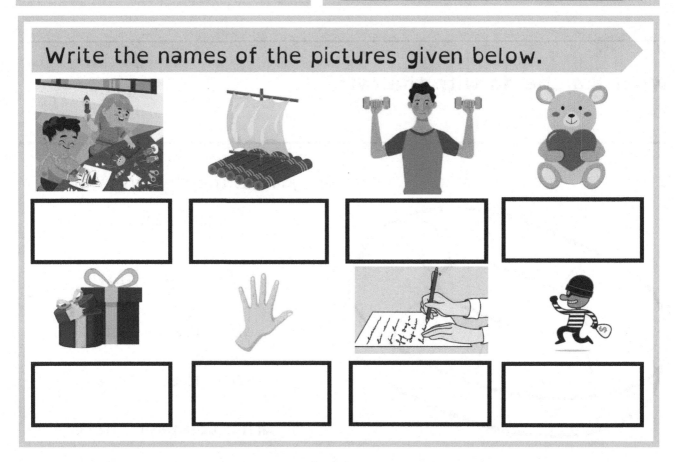

98

Rhymes with	Begins with
Loft	S_____
Drift	L_____
Shift	G_____
Cleft	L_____
Shaft	D_____
Left	T_____

Thomas and the Quilt

Thomas was a skilled tailor; he crafted a beautiful quilt with intricate patterns and patches of different colored fabrics. He left everyone speechless with his creation. His friend John who had built a tower in the town, came to Thomas. Suddenly, a storm appeared and lightning struck; the sewing machine halted abruptly. Thomas knelt to fix the machine. John inspected the machine and told Thomas that a loose belt had come off. Suddenly, Thomas looked at the quilt, and it had caught fire. The lightning had caused the candle to fall on the quilt, due to which it caught fire. Thomas felt guilt, as it was his fault. John consoled Thomas. After putting out the fire, he told him that he would make a much better quilt next time.

Thomas and the Quilt

Read the story and write all the 'lt' words found in the story.

Make sentences using the following words.

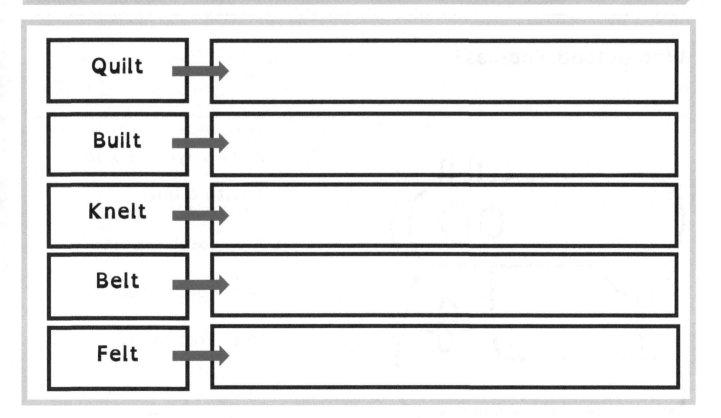

Quilt	
Built	
Knelt	
Belt	
Felt	

Thomas and the Quilt

What are the names of the characters in the story?

_____

What did Thomas do?

_____

What did John build?

_____

What happened to the quilt?

_____

Who helped Thomas?

_____

Join all the rhyming words with a line.

built   belt   bolt

melt   guilt   colt

felt   volt   quilt

knelt   tilt   revolt

102

Trace:

Say the word 3 times.

(1) (2) (3)

Draw a belt.

Find the 'lt' words.

b	r	a	h	t	s	f
e	w	i	a	t	a	e
l	e	f	l	p	l	l
t	a	c	t	g	t	t
q	u	i	l	t	s	p

Write the names of the pictures given below.

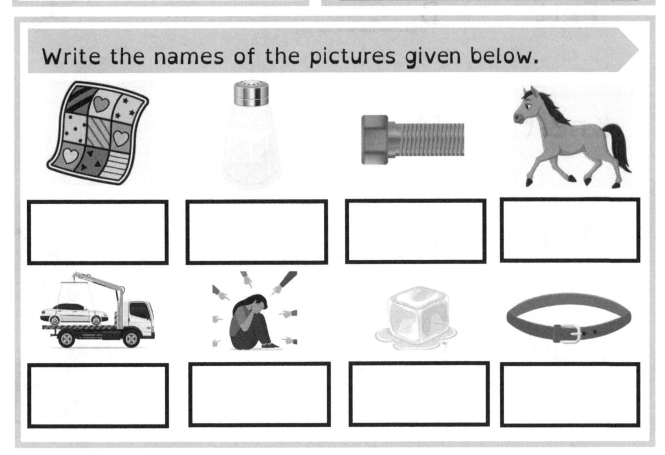

Rhymes with	Begins with
Bolt	C_____
Built	Q_____
Felt	B_____
Knelt	M_____
Tilt	G_____
Fault	S_____

The Traveler and the Saint

Once upon a time, a traveler was walking in the desert. He was panting heavily and was about to faint. A saint appeared out of nowhere and gave him a bottle of water. The traveler gulped the water and thanked the saint. The saint asked him to build a tent, as he was not in a condition to travel anymore. The saint helped him in making a tent. The saint lent him his water bottle and a paintbrush. The saint told the traveler if he would be in any problem, this paintbrush would pull him out of it. The traveler bent to pick up his bag and asked the saint to take care of him, then went outside the tent. The traveler followed the saint, but the saint had just vanished.

The Traveler and the Saint

Make sentences using the following words.

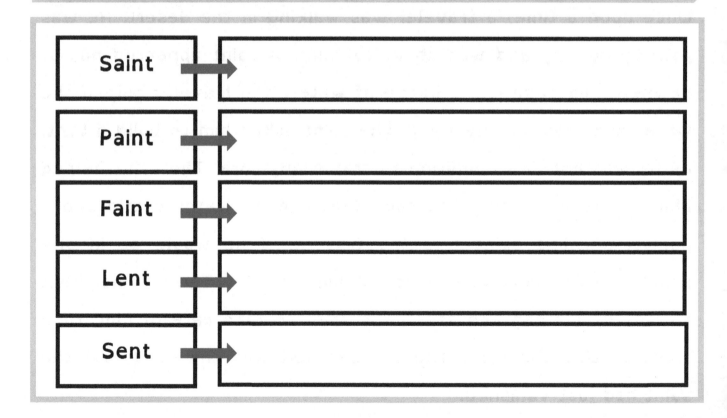

Saint	
Paint	
Faint	
Lent	
Sent	

The Traveler and the Saint

Where was the traveler walking?

_____

What did the saint give to the traveler?

_____

Who built the tent?

_____

Who helped the traveler when he was about to faint?

_____

What happened when the traveler went after the saint?

_____

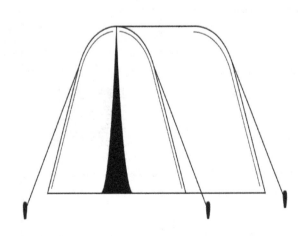

Join all the rhyming words

with a line.

saint   sent   tint

meant   faint   pint

pant   lint   paint

lent   flint   quaint

Trace:

paint

Say the word 3 times.

(1) (2) (3)

Draw a paint bucket.

Find the 'nt' words.

p	o	i	n	t	s	p
e	w	i	a	t	a	a
t	i	n		p	i	i
t	m	i	n	t	n	n
f	a	i	n	t	t	t

Write the names of the pictures given below.

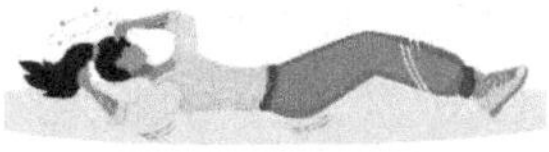

Rhymes with	Begins with
Rant	P_____
Meant	V_____
Can't	A_____
Lent	T_____
Paint	S_____
Rent	B_____

The Struggling Playwright

Maddison was a struggling playwright. She sought to adapt her script to the live audience. She was working on a play and tried to adopt a new approach that would sculpt her words into emotions. She spent days and nights sculpting her script to perfection. Sometimes, it was so hard for her that she wept at night. Despite all the doubt that crept in, she kept pushing herself. Finally, it was the day of the performance. She stood behind the curtains with great courage, and as the curtains rose, she witnessed a crowd staring at her. In the crowd there was a corrupt critique who tried to sabotage her work. She braced herself stronger and performed in front of the ocean of audience, who clapped at her work and admired her script. Her artistry was accepted with thunderous applause.

The Struggling Playwright

Read the story and write all the 'pt' words found in the story.

Make sentences using the following words.

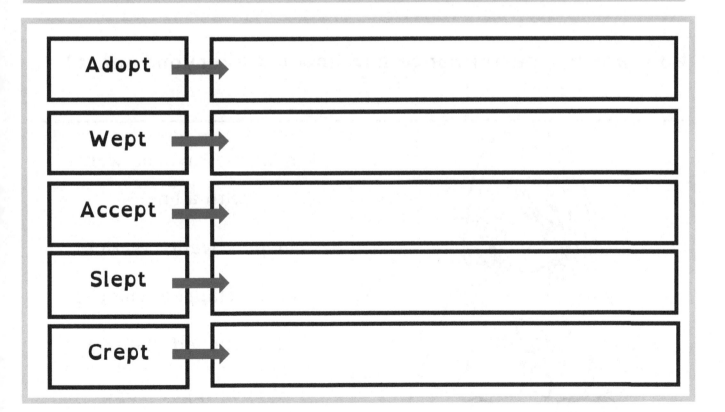

Adopt

Wept

Accept

Slept

Crept

The Traveler and the Saint

What was the girl's profession?

_____

What was the name of the girl?

_____

What was the girl working on?

_____

How did she reach perfection?

_____

How was her performance and how did everyone react?

_____

Join all the rhyming words with a line.

adapt   wept   script

swept   clapped   chipped

kept   clipped   flapped

slept   ripped   apt

Trace:

slept

Say the word 3 times.

(1) (2) (3)

Draw a sleeping cat.

Find the 'pt' words.

s	l	e	p	t	s	c
e	w	i	a	t	a	r
t	a	d	o	p	t	e
a	d	a	p	t	n	p
c	r	y	p	t	t	t

Write the names of the pictures given below.

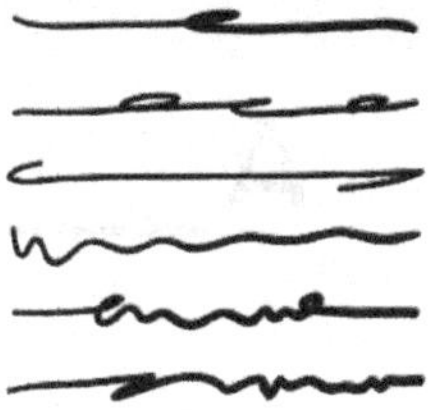

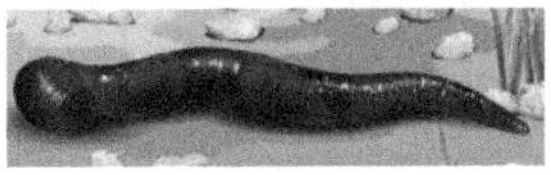

Rhymes with	Begins with
Kept	W_____
Abrupt	C_____
Clipt	C_____
Opt	A_____
Dysrupt	E_____
Crypt	S_____

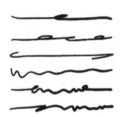

The Archer's Tale

Ronald was determined to become the best archer in his village. He would test his skills daily to participate in the annual archery competition. One day, while he was practicing, he saw a nest. He stopped and sat below the tree to rest and admire nature's beauty. Suddenly, a guest appeared and gave Ronald a vest. The guest himself was an archer and the best one anyone had ever seen. Ronald put on the vest and cast aside all the doubts he had. He went to the site of the competition and took part in it with a great sense of accomplishment. As the last round approached, he aimed at the targets on the list and hit each one of them in the bull's eye.

The Archer's Tale

Read the story and write all the 'st' words found in the story.

Make sentences using the following words.

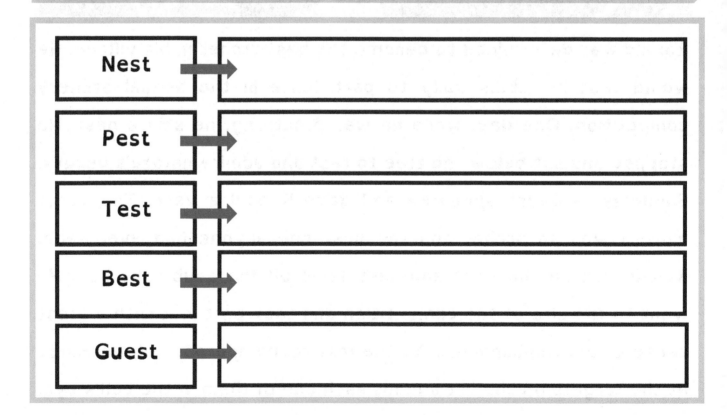

Nest	
Pest	
Test	
Best	
Guest	

116

The Archer's Tale

Answer the questions asked below.

What is the name of the boy?

_____

What was the boy practicing?

_____

Where did he want to compete?

_____

What did the guest give him?

_____

How did he perform at the competition?

_____

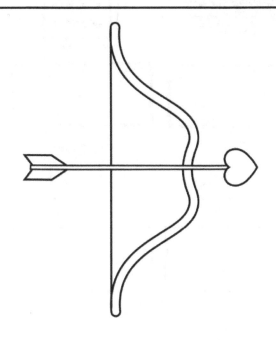

Join all the rhyming words
with a line.

nest   past   fist

last   pest   list

fast   cyst   test

myst   cast   rest

Trace:

nest

Say the word 3 times.

(1) (2) (3)

Draw a nest.

Find the 'st' words.

n	l	p	p	t	t	b
e	w	e	a	t	s	e
s	a	s	o	p	a	a
t	d	t	p	t	e	s
c	t	e	s	t	f	t

Write the names of the pictures given below.

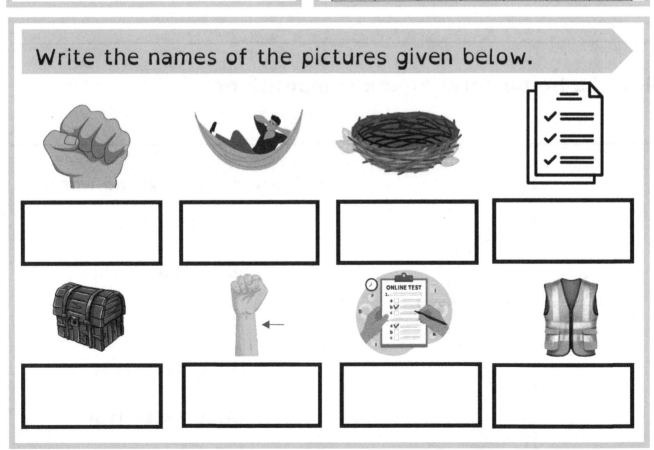

Write the word and match it with its rhyming picture.

Rhymes with	Begins with
Pest	V_____
Best	N_____
Fist	L_____
Crest	C_____
West	T_____
Guest	R_____

'ng' blends

(ng words)

The Melodious Tunes

Activities

Rhyming words	Questions and Answers	Story Reading	Find the Words
Pictures names	Matching Activity	Coloring Activity	Drawing Activity

Target Words

Fangs   bang   king   sing   long   tongs

lung   song

The Melodious Tunes

Once upon a time in a forest, lived a fierce tiger with sharp fangs, ready to strike. Suddenly, a loud bang was heard through the trees causing the king of the jungle to halt. The tiger was curious to know where the sound came from. He followed the voice and saw a group of monkeys who were singing in harmony. A monkey with nimble long fingers used tongs to play it as an instrument. The tiger's lungs filled with melody, and he couldn't help himself but dance. The tiger felt mesmerized hearing the melodious tunes and harmonious songs. All the animals gathered to dance and enjoy the tunes of music.

The Melodious Tunes

Read the story and write all the 'ng' words found in the story.

Make sentences using the following words.

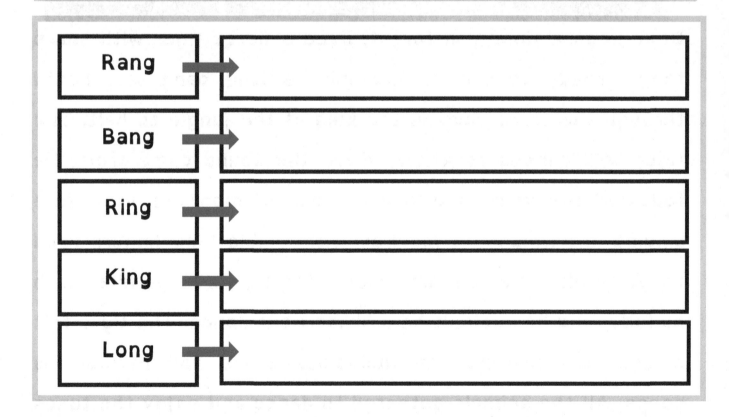

Rang	→
Bang	→
Ring	→
King	→
Long	→

The Melodious Tunes

Who was ready to strike?

_____

What stopped the tiger from striking?

_____

What did he see when he followed the voice?

_____

What happened when the tiger saw the monkeys singing?

_____

Who gathered in the jungle to enjoy the music?

_____

Join all the rhyming words
with a line.

ring   rang   lung

bang   sing   sung

rung   sang   bring

tongue   fang   fling

Trace:

ring

Say the word 3 times.

1 2 3

Draw a ring.

Find the 'ng' words.

l	s	o	n	g	r	r
u	e	l	l	g	i	a
n	s	k	o	n	n	n
g	a	c	n	i	g	g
b	a	n	g	s	s	p

Write the names of the pictures given below.

Rhymes with	Begins with
Rang	F_____
Sung	L_____
Wrong	T_____
Stung	L_____
Bing	R_____
Wing	S_____

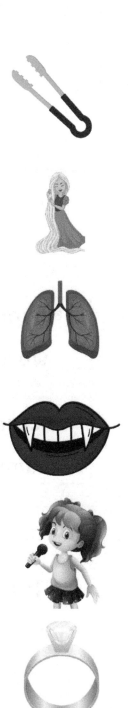

'nk' blends

(nk words)

Josh's
Masterpiece

Activities

| Rhyming words | Questions and Answers | Story Reading | Find the Words |
| Pictures names | Matching Activity | Coloring Activity | Drawing Activity |

Target Words

Ink   blink   sink   bank   plank   tank

honk   monk   skunk   trunk

Josh's Masterpiece

Josh was a writer; he dipped his pen into the ink to compose his next masterpiece. With each blink of an eye, ideas flowed through his mind. He was creating a masterpiece that would sink deep into the reader's soul. He had just withdrawn the money from the bank to buy a new wooden plank and a batch of pens. He placed the wooden plank on the broken table to write his story. Nearby, a tank was passing through with a continuous honk from its horn. Instead of being disturbed, Josh felt relaxed like a monk in meditation. Josh looked outside the window and saw a skunk scurrying through an abandoned old trunk. Josh closed the window and continued working on his masterpiece.

Josh's Masterpiece

Make sentences using the following words.

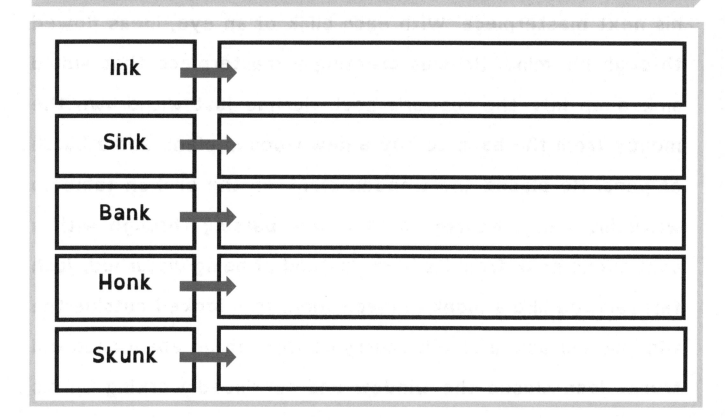

Josh's Masterpiece

What did Josh do?

_____

What was Josh working on?

_____

Why did he withdraw money from the bank?

_____

What passed through nearby?

_____

What did he see outside the window?

_____

Join all the rhyming words with a line.

ink   rank   trunk

tank   rink   skunk

sank   bunk   sink

blink   bank   flunk

129

Trace:

Say the word 3 times.

(1) (2) (3)

Draw a trunk.

Find the 'nk' words.

l	t	r	u	n	k	f
u	t	a	n	k	i	l
n	r	a	n	k	n	u
b	l	i	n	k	g	n
s	i	n	k	s	s	k

Write the names of the pictures given below.

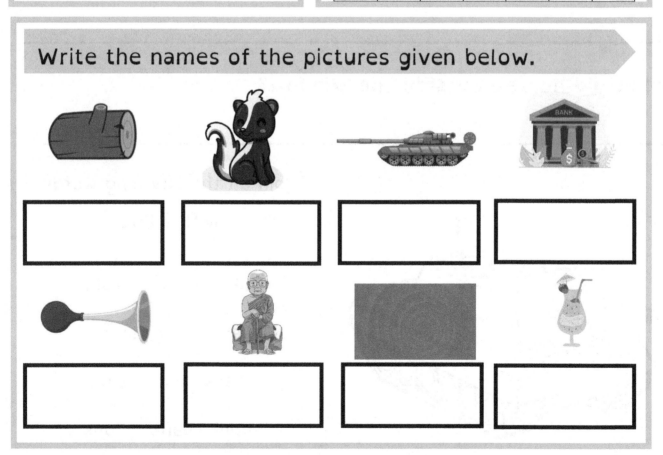

Write the word and match it with its rhyming picture.

Rhymes with	Begins with
Punk	M_ _ _ _ _ _
Bonk	H_ _ _ _ _
Rank	B_ _ _ _ _
Thank	T_ _ _ _ _
Chunk	S_ _ _ _ _
Bunk	T_ _ _ _ _

Made in United States
Orlando, FL
03 September 2024

51092757R00078